Adrian Fisher – Maze Designer

The Norton Museum of Art is very proud to host the exhibition, "An Ama─────────────────────isher, as part of its─────────────────────led facility, open─────────────────────

A─────────────────────oth indoors and ─────────────────────e, that his first one-─────────────────────um of Art, in West─────────────────────ew World, wher─────────────────────innovations in the art form. This exhibition includes the permanent installation of one of Adrian's "signature pieces" a 64 x 44 ft brick pavement maze of "Theseus and the Minotaur" in the Museum's East Garden, where Paul Manship's bronzes of Diana and Actaeon, installed in 1941, set a classical mythological note. Adrian's exhibition is running concurrently with a major exhibition of Rodin's sculpture. These two exhibitions pose intriguing contrasts and parallels. Both involve three-dimensional plastic reality, and engage the visitor in a mental dialogue. The difference is that with a maze, one can enter and interact physically with the piece, rather than just viewing as a simple observer. Once started, one must persevere until the puzzle is solved.

This exhibition is not only an example of the Museum's commitment to contemporary art, but also a recognition of the growing community. The Norton is an increasingly popular destination for schools and young families, which are new audiences in museum terms. We are pleased to have found in Adrian Fisher's work an exhibition which will stimulate and educate these younger audiences while providing an outlet for the abiding curiosity and love of art of more established museum visitors. We wish you a fascinating – and perhaps unexpectedly long! – visit to Adrian Fisher's exhibition of contemporary labyrinths.

Christina Orr-Cahall, Director, Norton Museum of Art, West Palm Beach, Florida, USA.

Adrian Fisher was born in Bournemouth, England, in 1951, the son of a doctor and the eldest of five children. They grew up in a large landscape garden, alongside the River Stour in Dorset, which was to be the site of his first hedge maze in 1975. Adrian travelled for a year in Australia, and then spent 8 years working in British industry, before starting his maze design business. His appreciation of landscape, his aptitude for mathematics and three-dimensional space, and his love of history and the arts, all combined to prepare him for his extraordinary vocation of designing and creating unique and beautiful mazes all over the world.

Mazes of the Earth

Ancient turf labyrinths from the Dark Ages and Medieval times still survive in the English landscape. When walking or running their paths, everyone on the labyrinth is drawn together in the experience, even if separated by time and distance on their individual journeys. Cut directly into the earth, without vertical barriers, these mazes inspire a powerful sensation of being in contact with Mother Earth.

The simplest form of earth maze is the traditional Turf Maze, cut directly into smooth grass, with the gullies forming the barriers, and the remaining grass appearing to have been raised up to form the paths.

Adrian pioneered the idea of reversing the role of the grass strip, by making it the barrier instead, and creating a firm path in brick or stone. In this way, the maze can be used by large numbers of visitors without wearing out the grass, yet the impression remains of walking on a grass lawn.

TOP OF PAGE: "Robin Hood's Race" Turf Maze at Lebanon Valley College, Annville, Pennsylvania. Adrian created this traditional turf maze in 24 hours as part of the first Amazing Maize Maze in 1993. Its turns and bastions proved intriguing to visitors, and its direct relationship with the Earth provided a satisfying contemplative journey.

ABOVE: Stone Labyrinth on a Beach in Wales. Adrian created this Classical seven-ring labyrinth on a steeply sloping beach in Wales, where smooth rounded stones and boulders were plentiful. The natural way to think of the design was with the entrance at the bottom, looking at the image up the slope. Over past centuries, similar thoughts must have crossed the minds of the creators of the 600 stone labyrinths still to be found along the shores of the Baltic Sea.

VERONICA'S MAZE

This quarter-mile maze of brick paths was built on the lawn where the owner Veronica Tritton used to play as a girl. Nowhere in the design is there a straight line, since the design was inspired by the ancient embroidery over the Great Bed in Parham House. This is a one-way maze; once you have started walking, you must keep going forwards, only taking gentle forks, but no sharp turns.

THE ARCHBISHOP'S MAZE

Between 1979 and 1986, Adrian Fisher designed 15 mazes together with Randoll Coate. This was their first collaboration.

Dr Robert Runcie, Archbishop of Canterbury, had described his dream of a maze in his enthronement sermon in 1980, and his words describing the human journey through life, and the need to build bridges between nations, were given physical expression at Greys Court in the Oxfordshire countryside. The maze abounds in Christian symbolism, with its cruciform shape, image of the Crown of Thorns, seven days of creation and twelve apostles.

Quite apart from the final result, the "act of creation" was highly significant to everyone involved, and Lady Brunner was just the first of many maze owners to revel in the creative process. It was her inspired idea to commission the maze, and she took a personal interest throughout, referring to the various craftsmen involved as her "band of brothers". For Adrian, it was the first time he had made his mark on a landscape, and he found his first impressions on seeing the 85 ft diameter circle cut into the sloping land profoundly moving.

BATH MAZE

"The Maze" was chosen as the theme of the 1984 Bath International Festival, and this path maze is its most enduring manifestation. A quarter mile of elliptical Bath stone paths lead to a central mosaic, 15 feet in diameter, made of 72,000 mosaic pieces. Within the mosaic, seven miniature Gaze Mazes invite the visitor to trace and solve them by eye. Each maze is also an image of an aspect of the history of the city, including the famous Gorgon's head of Bath.

TOP OF PAGE: Veronica's Maze, Parham Park, West Sussex, England (designed by Adrian Fisher & Lesley Beck, 1991).

ABOVE CENTRE: Archbishop's Maze, Greys Court, Oxfordshire, England (designed by Adrian Fisher & Randoll Coate, 1981).

ABOVE: Bath Maze, Beazer Gardens, Bath, England (Fisher & Coate, 1984).

Your land is his Canvas

BELOW: Sequence of Alice-in-Wonderland Maze being built.

To create an image directly onto the surface of the earth has been an enduring human endeavour from pre-history to the present day. Examples survive from many cultures ranging from creatures drawn on the Nazca plain in Peru to white horses carved into the English chalk downs.

In his work Adrian Fisher is continuing this ancient tradition using the land as his canvas, drawing directly onto the landscape. In common with other forms of land art, the physical construction of the maze is an important and fulfilling part of the creative process. In order to achieve the high degree of accuracy demanded by such precise and complex designs, Adrian frequently works with a team of specialist landscape contractors and personally directs the marking out of each maze.

There is a unique quality to the character of a formal hedge maze. The tall clipped hedges form a puzzle on a grand scale, with nature itself harnessed to confound human comprehension. Symbolic of mankind's taming of the wilderness, hedge mazes have a long history in European formal gardens. Using his expert knowledge of this history to inform his designs, Adrian has created many of the most spectacular contemporary hedge mazes in Britain and Europe. Each maze evokes the formal hedge maze tradition without losing its connection with contemporary culture. He has produced both figurative and abstract designs, each carefully researched to have particular relevance to the location.

The design of the Saxon Maze at The Herb Farm, Sonning Common, Berkshire, England (Fisher & Beck 1991) is based on the depiction of four mythical sea creatures in an eighth century illuminated manuscript. The maze has a four fold rotational symmetry that reflects the four main categories of herbs: culinary, medicinal, aromatic and decorative. Visitors to the maze reach the eye of each creature to discover the four sacred Saxon herbs before reaching the central tump from where the whole maze can be viewed.

ABOVE LEFT: Leeds Castle Maze, England (Adrian Fisher, Randoll Coate and Vernon Gibberd 1988).

ABOVE: Newquay Zoo, England (Fisher & Coate, 1984).

A Maze for Discovery

The Darwin Maze at Edinburgh Zoo was formally opened by Her Royal Highness Princess Anne in 1995. Conceived as an experiential interpretation of Darwin's theory of Evolution and the Origin of Species this interactive hedge maze takes the form of the famous Galapagos giant tortoise.

By the use of this bold zoomorphic form this maze once more makes the connection with ancient geoglyphs, evocations of the animal gods, whilst its potent symbolism reminds the visitor of the underlying ecological message of the maze.

As visitors walk through the maze, they encounter the conditions required for evolution; two genders, abundant offspring, predators, natural selection, parting of species, distinct breeding groups, and origin of new species. The interpretation of the subject is both informative and amusing, enhancing the maze puzzle with interactive features. For example in the Chamber of Natural Selection progress is blocked by foaming fountain gates; electronic beams test certain personal characteristics, which may be weight, colour or smell, although which one is being tested is not revealed. If the right characteristics are detected, the fountain gates fall to allow passage onwards. If your characteristics are unfavourable, then you become extinct and another fountain gate opens taking you back to the start. Life is cruel!

The Darwin Maze also contains two large-scale decorative brick pavements. The first, which forms a border terrace, is a one hundred foot long version of the DNA spiral, and the second, at the centre of the maze itself, portrays an Oran Utang, twenty feet square. These colourful tessellations are constructed from Adrian's unique polygonal clay paver shapes. The Oran Utang design, created by Adrian Fisher and Jacqueline Bishop, is also a pavement maze in its own right. The three-dimensional nature of the maze is enhanced by the inclusion of wooden bridges which allow an overview of the maze, access to other parts of the puzzle and a quick exit. To further enhance the interactive nature of the maze for the large numbers of children who visit the zoo, a quiz trail is included. This involves collecting the answers to a set of educational questions on the theme of evolution by visiting all the different parts of the maze.

ABOVE: Aerial view of The Darwin Maze at Edinburgh Zoo, Scotland (Adrian Fisher, 1995).

The world's first Multi-Sensory Maze was built to teach personal mobility to the blind and partially-sighted students of RNIB New College, Worcester, England. The maze contains 14 different kinds of maze walls, 14 different path surfaces, 6 fountains, 2 bridges, a tunnel, a central tower with spiral staircase, a herb garden, a chess garden and a colour maze.

Maze for the Blind

The Multi-Sensory Mobility Maze for the Blind was built during 1993 at New College in Worcester, Britain's premier secondary school of the Royal National Institute for the Blind. This maze provides a safe training environment for blind and partially-blind students to practice moving around in a confusing and dangerous world. Students and mobility teachers were consulted in its conception and design and the mobility teachers consider the maze to provide three years of useful training exercises.

For maximum variety, the maze has fourteen different kinds of vertical barriers, and fourteen different path surfaces. These include brick walls, cast-iron railings, hedges, wooden fencing, paths of gravel, concrete pavers, shredded bark and tarmac. In certain areas a series of different surfaces are laid closely together, to form a Texture Alley. Training opportunities include a section of brick wall with four gaps in it to enable the students to be trained to detect the gaps without touching, mainly by different sound echoes, and partly by changes in air pressure on the face. Growing hedges provide minimal echo and are more difficult to detect than walls or fences.

Various changes in levels are provided, with two bridges, a central tower, ramps, and the edge of a railway station platform. The bridges have handrails at the correct height to give practice going up and down unfamiliar stairs.

Sound can be used to help understand surroundings so the maze contains a metal tunnel filled with crunchy shingle, and a length of giant concrete pipe which produce superb echoes.

The sound of water can be confusing as well as intriguing so two rows of foaming fountain gates bar the way in different parts of the maze, rising and falling at random intervals. Once found, there is the fun of feeling the water jets by hand, and feeling the extra moisture in the surrounding air.

Only two percent of blind people have no sight at all so for those with a measure of sight the "Adonis Blue Butterfly" Colour Maze made of bright plastic tiles was included. The colour scheme was designed to provide sharp contrast, rather than the congenial colours that appeal more to the fully-sighted.

A fragrant Herb Garden and a Chess Garden with giant pieces on a textured chequer board add elements of play and relaxation. Finally, this is a proper puzzle maze, with a central tower to be reached, a goal to be found, and a quick exit. Seen from the air, the design portrays five Poker Dice in a box, a King and four Aces.

The Maze for the Blind also contains statues and sculpture, a telephone kiosk, a post box, a fully functioning Pelican Crossing, and one and a half cars.
From the air, the design portrays 5 Poker Dice –
4 Aces and a King.
Part of the challenge was to build the whole maze in 72 hours, and its construction was the subject of a 50 minute British television programme in October 1993 (designed by Adrian Fisher, 1993).

Brick Pavement Mazes

Adrian regards natural clay brick as a superb paving medium, with its rich colours and textures, which lends itself wonderfully for mazes both as decorative features within a larger paving scheme as well as for play. A paving maze creates an oasis of activity thus making the chosen area a special focus for play and social interaction. As with all paving projects, maze design requires careful consideration of the precise method of paver laying, paver type and colour, wearing characteristics, level of craftsmanship required, cost and the time available for installation. His own material library includes every clay paver on the UK market, with over thirty vibrant colours represented. These are carefully colour matched to the graphic designers' Pantone colour palette, allowing computer-generated designs to be prepared which are accurately colour-matched in advance. After producing his initial design concept by hand the brick by brick final layout is designed on a state-of-the-art computer package ensuring the complete accuracy that this medium demands.

BELOW: Lion Rampant Maze, Worksop England (Fisher, Beck & Coate, 1990). The Lion Rampant and Unicorn Rampant pavement mazes were the keynote features within the new pedestrian precinct in Worksop Town Centre, which was the outright winner of Britain's "Street Design '90" award.

LEFT: Mary Hare Grammar School
This new 6th Form courtyard at **Mary Hare Grammar School** for the Deaf, Newbury, England contains a giant seashell spiral in clay cobbles. As well as being a pavement maze, it is also a visual pun on a labyrinth of the inner ear. The design for the whole courtyard garden features some of the many opportunities offered by decorative paving. (Adrian Fisher 1995).

ABOVE: Maze Courtyard at Elson Junior School, Gosport, Hampshire, England (designed by Adrian Fisher 1996). In July 1996, Adrian created a playground brick pavement with two mazes at **Elson Junior School,** in Gosport, Hampshire, England. The paving was designed to fit around seven existing trees. The innovative design features his "Random Basket-Weave Paving" for the first time.

ABOVE: Maze Courtyard at St. Johns School, Moordown, Bournemouth, England (designed by Adrian Fisher, 1996). This vigorous maze courtyard at **St John's School, Moordown**, Bournemouth in Dorset, England, Adrian's old junior school, was laid out on a paving grid at 45 degrees to the alignment of the courtyard. The school's logo takes centre stage, and the halo of the Lamb was made with rings of clay cobbles. Interestingly, a pavement maze provides compelling repeat play value throughout the school year, even though it is always being used by the same finite number of pupils.

Paving Inventions

BELOW: Computer artwork for Reptile paving (Adrian Fisher 1996).

FOOT OF PAGE: Oran Utang in a burning rainforest, Darwin Maze, Edinburgh Zoo, Scotland (designed by Adrian Fisher & Jacqueline Bishop, 1995).

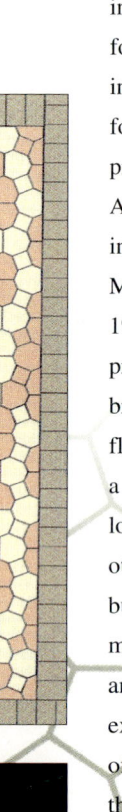

Adrian's fascination with patterns and their mathematical and aesthetic possibilities have inspired him to pioneer many forms of decorative paving including many new tessellations for brick paving. These can produce some sensational effects. An excellent example of his innovative approach is the Darwin Maze at Edinburgh Zoo, opened in 1995 by Princess Anne. This project includes two decorative brick pavements both laid on a flexible base construction. One is a regular terrace, forty metres long, depicting a DNA spiral. The other portrays an Oran Utang in a burning rainforest, symbolising mankind destroying his habitat, and in this way threatening extinction. This was the first use of a new tessellation technique that Adrian invented using specially made pavers. The shaped units are five and seven sided pieces which fit together in an infinite variety of patterns. Adrian has also invented a new series of exciting tessellations using different combinations of multi sided polygons.

Water Inventions

BELOW: Labyrinthe des Dragons, Peaugres Safari Park, France (Adrian Fisher & Francois Blanc, 1994): Walk-Through Parting Waterfall

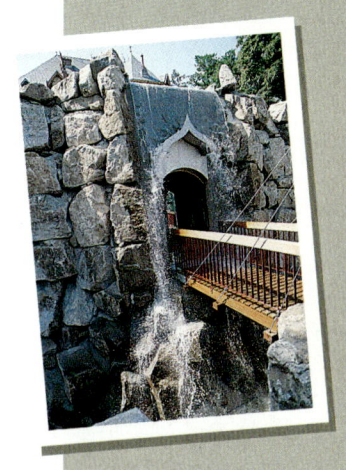

CENTRE RIGHT: Legoland, Windsor, England (Adrian Fisher & Gillespies, 1996): Waterfall closed.

LOWER RIGHT: Legoland, Windsor, England (Adrian Fisher & Gillespies, 1996): Waterfall open.

Not content with creating fascinating puzzle mazes on a grand scale Adrian's obsession with innovation has drawn him to re-assess the dramatic possibilities of the maze in a contemporary context. Some of his most effective inventions involve water, used to fascinate and surprise.

Adrian's invention of the Walk-Through Parting Waterfall is both a great joke and a dramatic entrance to the mystery of a maze. The waterfall would look silly without a majestic rockface or castle entrance behind it. The water then needs to fall into a proper pool. In turn the pool becomes an obstacle requiring a footbridge to cross it. This absurd feature now creates its own absurd problem, since the waterfall is blocking the path. Fortunately as each visitor crosses the bridge, the water magically parts for a few seconds, and they quicken their pace and hasten across for fear of getting soaked. It's another example of Adrian's concept of "VW" (Virtual Wetness) where you nearly get seriously wet but actually you stay dry, and come away feeling incredibly brave.

In the same spirit Adrian created his Foaming Fountain Gates to add yet another layer of puzzlement to a maze. These one metre high foaming spouts rise or fall from the ground to block or open the path. Some are controlled by random switches and other by electronic systems which detect certain characteristics in the participants. In this way the layout of the maze can change interactively giving each person an individual journey through the labyrinth.

Portable Colour Mazes

Adrian Fisher's Colour Mazes first appeared in Scientific American magazine in 1984. Made up of thousands of interlocking coloured plastic tiles they become complex mazes based on bold graphic images. They are like regular puzzle mazes in many ways having an entrance, a goal, numerous paths, and junctions with choices to make. However, they are more difficult to solve, because each one has a simple extra rule to obey.

This can involve taking paths in a particular colour sequence, following directional arrows or using a particular number pattern which indicates the precise distance to be taken in a given direction. In some of the designs only forward movement is allowed and others conform to an alphabetical or mathematical system, some to the moves of chess pieces. Altogether Adrian has devised over a dozen fascinating and mind-stretching ways of moving around and solving Colour Mazes.

BELOW: San Antonio Children's Museum, Texas, USA (Adrian Fisher, 1996). This custom designed Colour Maze of "Two Grey Hills" was based on a native indian rug design. Echoed within the design of the maze is a thin thread that stretches from the right corner around the edge of the rug. In Pueblos tradition, this thread is placed there to let the "spirit of the rug" come and go through the woven border unhindered.

LEFT: Louisiana Children's Museum, New Orleans, Louisiana, USA (Adrian Fisher, 1993). Colour Mazes are excellent for promoting a corporate identity. This colour maze is based on the logo of the Louisiana Children's Museum. The puzzle is to enter at one of the two doors, travel from window to window, and finally reach the Moon – never using the same path colour twice consecutively. It's not as easy as it looks.

RIGHT: "Circle 8" Colour Maze in a shady courtyard in Savannah, Georgia, USA (Adrian Fisher, 1994). The ambience of the setting, and the physical scale of the surroundings, can have a very powerful influence on the quality of play. In this intimate shady courtyard, these Montessori children played on the Colour Maze for half an hour, each solving the maze puzzle, and then discussing and devising interactive games of their own invention to play on the maze. Some games involved Co-operation, whilst others were more Competitive. Less intimate settings do not sustain such prolonged play.

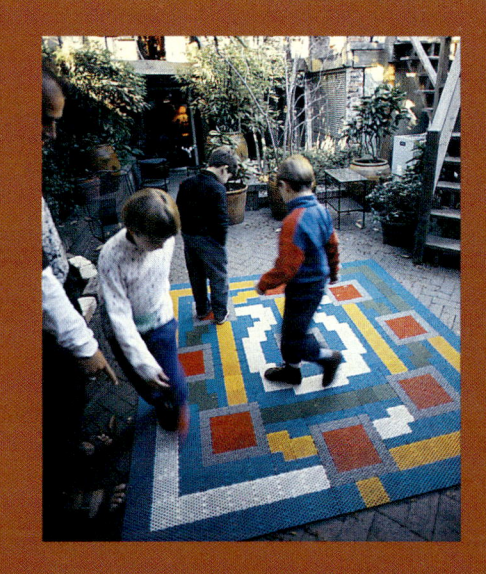

LEFT: "Star 21" Colour Maze for New York Hall of Science, New York, USA (Adrian Fisher, 1993). Its lively colours act as a magnet to children, as well as being instantly recognisable as a maze. This maze can be played in three ways; as a traditional puzzle maze, ignoring the coloured paths, as a Dual-Colour Maze, changing path colour from Yellow to White, or from White to Yellow, each time you reach a Red Decision Square, or as a Processional Labyrinth, reaching each Red junction once and once only.

RIGHT: "Arrow 25" Maze on a cruise ship, Tampa, Florida, USA (designed by Adrian Fisher, 1993). Portable Colour Mazes can be used in a wide range of locations, including even the decks of cruise liners. This arrow maze involves moving varying distances, each time in the direction indicated by the arrow on which you land.

Mirror Mazes

In a mirror maze, the deceptions are not so much physical dead ends, as visual illusions of impossible paths, mixed with the possible paths. A mirror maze appears three or four times larger inside than it measures on the outside, giving the illusion of spacious, pillar-lined, avenues in all directions forming an endless collonade. The underlying geometry avoids right angles, therefore achieving unexpected reflections at every turn.

ABOVE LEFT: Magical Mirror Maze, Wookey Hole Caves, Somerset, England (designed by Adrian Fisher and Lesley Beck, 1991). Which of the four figures is the real photographer?! This is one of the world's finest mirror mazes, with large high-quality mirrors, hidden deceptions, spectacular lighting effects, and a central fountain with over 100 jets which dance to the tonal variations of the music.

ABOVE: Labyrinthe des Dragons, Peaugres Safari Park, France (designed by Adrian Fisher and Francois Blanc, 1994). Taking its theme from the Great Labyrinth of Ancient Egypt this mirror maze contains live crocodiles, pythons, scorpions and bats, as well as tanks of aquarium fish behind the glass walls.

Maze of Motor Cars

Adrian's unique design talents find wide expression in our contemporary culture. This ranges from garden festivals and television game shows, to designing new forms of urban bus maps, paving brick systems, three dimensional pyramid puzzles, card games, printed card mazes, tapestry kits and T-shirt designs. A renowned expert on the history and theory of mazes he has written several books, and is a regular contributor to television and radio programs, newspapers and journals.

ABOVE: The Beatles' Maze, Liverpool, England. (Awarded 2 Gold Medals; designed by Adrian Fisher, Randoll Coate and Graham Burgess, 1984).

One of the world's most extraordinary mazes was created using 250 Rover motor cars, laid out as a puzzle maze, for the British TV programme "You Bet!". The British precision driver, Russ Swift, drove at speeds of up to 45 miles per hour including high-speed reversing, handbrake turns and 180° spins, attempting to travel through the maze in under $2^1/_2$ minutes.

Characteristically, Adrian's design had a sting in its tail. When Russ reached the far end, 8 of the cars were moved, thus presenting him with a different maze puzzle for his return trip. Russ succeeded in completing his challenge with just 2 seconds to spare. Despite an 18ft long car and just 22ft wide alleys, not a single car was scratched.

No celebration of Liverpool during its 1984 International Garden Festival would have been complete without reference to the Beatles. The Beatles' Maze with its giant Yellow Submarine as the goal and psychedelic Water Garden was the inspired result. The all-steel submarine weighed 18 tons, measured 51 feet long and was built by apprentices from the nearby dockyards where British naval submarines had been built for generations. Inside it contained genuine submarine equipment and twin spiral staircases leading up and down the conning tower to give an overview of the maze. Over a million people visited the Beatles' Maze within six months.

The largest mazes in the world

RIGHT: Golden Hinde, Shippensburg, Pennsylvania, USA (Adrian Fisher, 1995).

BELOW: Stegosaurus, Anneville, Pennsylvania, USA (Adrian Fisher, 1993). In September 1993, the largest maze in the world was created in a maize cornfield at Lebanon Valley College, Annville, Pennsylvania. This Amazing Maize Maze was 500 feet long, had over two miles of paths, and covered 126,000 square feet. Since it was 1993 and the year of the film Jurassic Park, Adrian designed the maze in the shape of a giant Stegosaurus. Over a warm sunny long weekend, 6,000 visitors raised $32,000 for the Red Cross Appeal for the Flood Victims of the Midwest.

Adrian Fisher's maze designs display a wide diversity of styles, materials and complexity. One other factor plays an essential part in his conception of the maze experience and that is scale. In common with other three-dimensional art forms the power of the concept is often intensified by considered use of scale. In terms of a colour maze it is the compact frame that concentrates the focus of a demanding solution. In some mazes, however, it is the sheer size of the maze that enhances the experience.

The Amazing Maize Mazes™ which Adrian has created with Broadway Producer Don Frantz are just that, enormous mazes created out of fields of maize corn. Each of these mazes that Adrian has designed has been an oversize land drawing representing the theme made by cutting the pathways within the living cornfield. Each maze design provides the arena where Don and his team develop the remarkable Creative Entertainment which has become such a hallmark of these Amazing Maize Mazes. This includes a Maze Master in a tall tower who communicates with visitors through speaking tubes giving advice and encouragement, specially composed music broadcast through a multi-speaker PA system, puzzle trails and games, giant flags for each family to take around the maze, and much more. Adrian and Don's Amazing Maize Mazes have broken the Guinness record for the world's largest maze, no fewer than three times.

Locomotive

In the suburb of Dearborn within the city of Detroit, Adrian and Don created the Quadricycle Maze, once again achieving the largest maze in the world, in the shape of Henry Ford's 1896 motorised "Quadricycle", to raise funds for Cancer Research. The resulting maze, covering over six acres and over a quarter of a million square feet, gained coast-to-coast TV coverage on the ABC network, and international coverage on CNN. For 1996, the specially composed musical score perfectly added to the spirit of the cornfield, using a total of 42 outdoor speakers to reach all parts of the giant maze. Three long wooden bridges added to the confusion of its giant three-dimensional puzzle. Inovations for 1996, were a rope Maze, and a Meditation Maze that was built half in turf and half within the cornfield.

In Pennsylvania, the Locomotive Labyrinth was created on Jack and Donna Coleman's farm right alongside the tracks of the Strasburg Railroad, which runs steam trains as a tourist attraction, in Lancaster County, the heart of the Amish Country. As before, the maze was reproduced as a T-shirt design. The nearest town is Paradise, a fitting name for this beautiful part of America. The site included a Racing Rope Maze and a Processional Maze that was built half in turf and half within the cornfield. Arrival and departure by Steam Train completed the experience.

The Amazing Maize Mazes are a great team effort, with Don Frantz (Show Producer), Adrian Fisher (Maze Designer), Allen Frantz and Rick Stepanchek (Production) and Diane Frantz (Administration) backed by a cast of many dozens more.

ABOVE: Locomotive Labyrinth as seen from the ground, Paradise, Pennsylvania, USA (Adrian Fisher 1996).

ABOVE LEFT: Locomotive Labyrinth from the air.

Wooden Mazes

Wooden Mazes provide an instant finished result, since they can be built in just a few weeks. Wooden fences are thin compared with hedges, so a wooden maze can provide an excellent puzzle in a compact area. Wooden panels can be stained the same colour or varying colours, according to the intended character of the maze. Adrian finds Wooden Mazes allow for highly ingenious three-dimensional puzzle mazes, since wooden bridges only need short decks to cross over several paths. To this, Adrian often likes to add the fourth dimension of Time, using Walk-Through Parting Waterfalls and Foaming Fountain Gates to add complexity.

BELOW: Merlin's Magical Maze, Holywell Bay, Cornwall, England (designed by Adrian Fisher, 1994). This Maze has red and green panels and is entered through a Parting Waterfall.

ABOVE: Maze of the Planets, East Tawas, Mitchigan, USA (designed by Adrian Fisher, 1994). This giant maze, 250 feet long, portrays the planet Saturn when seen from the sky. Four wooden bridges give the added impression of its giant rings passing in front of the planet.